# THE HIPPOLYTUS
## OF EURIPIDES

# THE
# HIPPOLYTUS
## OF EURIPIDES

★

*a translation by*

REX WARNER

WITHDRAWN

THE BODLEY HEAD · LONDON

First published 1949

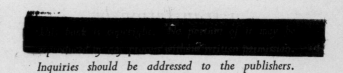

Inquiries should be addressed to the publishers.

Printed in Great Britain by
WESTERN PRINTING SERVICES LTD., BRISTOL
for THE BODLEY HEAD LIMITED
8 Bury Place London WC1

# THE CHARACTERS

★

THESEUS, *king of Athens*

HIPPOLYTUS, *his son*

PHAEDRA, *wife of Theseus*

APHRODITE
ARTEMIS } *two rival goddesses*

ATTENDANT *to Hippolytus*

NURSE *to Phaedra*

SERVANT

MESSENGER

CHORUS OF THE WOMEN OF TROEZEN

ATTENDANTS

# *Introduction*

★

ALTHOUGH the main elements of the plot of HIPPOLYTUS are set out in the first speech, or prologue, some knowledge of the background of the characters is still valuable for the understanding of the play.

Theseus, king of Athens, was the son, according to some legends of Aigeus, according to others of Poseidon, the god of the sea. Among his many exploits in youth was the carrying off of Antiope, sister of the Queen of the Amazons. Hippolytus was the son of Theseus and Antiope. He was brought up in Troezen by Pittheus, father of Theseus' mother Aethra.

Later Theseus married Phaedra, daughter of Minos, king of Crete. The family, apart from Minos himself, was notorious for extravagant or unhappy love affairs. Phaedra's mother was Pasiphae who, after her passion for the bull, gave birth to the Minotaur which was finally killed by Theseus. Her sister was Ariadne who, after falling in love with Theseus, and being deserted by him, was carried away by Dionysus. By Phaedra Theseus had two sons who, in the play, are alluded to as 'true-born', Hippolytus himself being regarded as illegitimate.

Hippolytus, as is clear from his first appearance in the play, is the devoted worshipper of the virgin goddess Artemis. He is even privileged to hear her voice and feel her presence while he is hunting. Wholly devoted to her, he has no time or inclination for the rival and opposite deity, Aphrodite, who decides to revenge herself on him for his neglect of her. The means she chooses are to make Phaedra fall in love with him, and to present Theseus with a false picture of what has happened, so that he will call down on Hippolytus one of the curses which his father Poseidon has empowered him to make. Hippolytus will be killed and Phaedra, though entirely innocent, will, in order to involve Hippolytus in ruin, take her own life.

On the face of it such a story might seem to be an attack on 'the ways of God to men' of the kind which Euripides does make sometimes, though not nearly so often as is commonly thought. He has been called a rationalist and a free-thinker, and in a sense the descriptions are justified. But his 'rationalism' is not in the least like Shaw's and his 'free thought' is always conscious of the wider boundaries of the poetic imagination.

In this play it is quite true that the attitude of Aphrodite, if we regard her as a real person, must appear as mean, savage, unscrupulous—anything but divine. There seems also to be a manifest inefficiency in the divine ordering of things when we discover that Artemis, a goddess of equal power with Aphrodite, can do nothing to preserve her innocent and trusting favourite—nothing except promise that in the end, by causing the death of Adonis, she will get even with her rival. Yet it must not be assumed that, because, by human standards, the gods in this play behave badly, therefore Euripides was writing irreligiously or with any notion of 'debunking' popular belief.

His purpose is certainly a wider one than this, and his goddesses are used as symbols to define and circumscribe a human problem. The problem is a familiar one in Greek tragedy. It is of the dangers involved in any kind of self-security or pride, and of the existence of powers which are more effective and perhaps, in the last resort, higher than justice. Hippolytus, like Prometheus, is innocent; yet, in his intense concentration on one aspect of reality, he is also guilty. It is not quite that he is too good, but that, by failing to appreciate other forces which exist, he sins by pride. His own virgin ideals may certainly seem higher ones than are the wholly physical and emotional claims which are made for love in the play. But the point is that Hippolytus will not even admit that such things exist. Though by no stretch of imagination can he be said to have deserved his fate, yet his fate is an example of something which happens. It is a heroic fate and the audience who saw the play performed in Athens in the year 428 B.C. would be aware that across the water in Troezen Hippolytus was still worshipped as a hero, and that in front of his tomb girls still before their marriage made offerings of the tresses of their hair.

It is interesting to recall that out of Euripides' seventy-five plays this was one of the five that received a first prize at the Athenian dramatic festival. It was produced just after the great plague of Athens in which, among many others, Pericles lost his life. The very last lines of the play are held, with some reason, to have been taken by the audience as a reference to this great statesman's death.

# THE HIPPOLYTUS
## OF EURIPIDES

★

[The scene is in Troezen, in front of
the palace of King Theseus. By the gates
are two statues one of Aphrodite and one
of Artemis. The goddess Aphrodite speaks.]

### APHRODITE

STRONG am I among mortals, not without a name,
the goddess Cypris, who in heaven too is known.
And of those who live and look upon the light of the sun
from Pontus to the boundaries that Atlas set,
I give honour to the ones who reverence my power,
and those whose thoughts of me are arrogant I crush.
You will find this holds even among the gods above:
they too are pleased when they receive the praise of men.
And I will show at once that what I say is true.
The son of Theseus from the Amazon his wife,
Hippolytus, brought up by Pittheus, that saintly man,
alone of all the people in this land, Troezen,
considers me the least important of the gods,
spurns love making and will not join in an embrace.
Instead he worships Phoebus' sister, Artemis,
the child of Zeus, and thinks her greatest of the gods,
and always with the virgin goddess in green woods
he clears the land of beasts with his swift hunting dogs,
in mightier company than that of human kind.

All this I do not grudge him. Why indeed should I?
But for sinning against me, upon this very day
I shall take vengeance on Hippolytus. The work
is begun already; there is not much left to do.
For once he came to Athens from the house of Pittheus
to see and to receive the holy mysteries,
and then his father's noble and respected wife,
Phaedra, first saw him, and she found her heart in the grip
of savage passion. This was as I planned it for her.
And before she came into this land of Troezen,
she built upon the rock of Pallas, looking out
over this land, a temple to me, the Cyprian.
Her love was absent, but it was for him she made
the temple and afterwards she called it by his name.
And now that Theseus, fleeing from the stain of blood
of Pallas' murdered sons, has taken on himself
one year of foreign exile and has left the land
of Cecrops and has sailed to this land with his wife,
now she, poor woman, wastes away in agony,
and, driven from her senses by the stings of love,
suffers in silence. No one with her knows her pain.
But this is not the way this love of hers must end.
I shall let Theseus know of it. All will come out.
Then this young man, my enemy, will be destroyed
by the curses of his father; for the lord of the sea,
Poseidon, gave to Theseus as an honoured right
that he should pray three times and have his prayer fulfilled.
As for the woman, Phaedra, she shall keep her name,
but none the less shall die. I shall not think her pain
of enough importance to prevent my enemies
from suffering the punishment that I think fit.
But now I see the son of Theseus coming here,
Hippolytus, fresh from his hunting exercise.
I therefore shall be gone. Behind him comes a great

and merry band of hunters, singing to Artemis,
hymning the goddess's praise. He does not know the gates
of Hell are open and this day he sees his last.

[*Aphrodite goes out. Hippolytus, carrying a garland in his hand, enters
followed by his attendants.*]

HIPPOLYTUS

Sing, as you follow me, sing of her
    heavenly daughter of Zeus,
Artemis, in whose care we are.

ATTENDANTS [*singing*]

Most holy lady, we worship you,
    child of the Highest.
We worship you, Lady Artemis,
Leto and Zeus's daughter.

You most beautiful far among
    maidens, you who in heaven dwell
    in the space of your father's court,
    in the golden palace of Zeus,
    hear us, most beautiful
    maid among maidens in heaven, most
    beautiful, Artemis.

[*Hippolytus advances to the statue of Artemis in front of the palace.*]

HIPPOLYTUS

For you, my lady, I have made and bring to you
this wreath of twined flowers from a virgin meadow,
a place where never shepherd thought to feed his flocks
nor ever came the stroke of iron. Instead the bees
cross and recross this virgin meadow in the spring.

13

And native Shame waters the ground with river dew,
and from his garden only those may pluck the flowers
who were elect from birth by a wise purity
in all things, and never had to learn it. Evil men
have no right there. And so, dear lady, take from this
reverent hand a binding for your golden hair.
For I alone of men am so distinguished as to be
constantly with you and to speak and hear your words.
I hear the voice, but I have never seen your face.
O, let me end my life as I have started it!

[*One of his attendants approaches him.*]

ATTENDANT

Sir, for 'master' is a word I use for gods—
if I gave good advice, would you receive it from me?

HIPPOLYTUS

Of course I would. It would be stupid not to do so.

ATTENDANT

Do you know of a rule that is general among men?

HIPPOLYTUS

What rule? What is it you are telling me about?

ATTENDANT

People hate pride and an exclusive attitude.

HIPPOLYTUS

Quite right. An arrogant person is always hated.

ATTENDANT

And people are grateful when you talk to them kindly.

14

**HIPPOLYTUS**

Certainly. It does much good, and costs little trouble.

**ATTENDANT**

And do you think that the same thing is true of gods?

**HIPPOLYTUS**

Yes, since we mortals live by the same rules as they.

**ATTENDANT**

Then why do you not say a word to a great goddess?

**HIPPOLYTUS**

Which one? Be careful that you name what can be named.

**ATTENDANT**

The one that stands there. The Cyprian at your gates.

**HIPPOLYTUS**

Since I live cleanly, I greet her from a distance.

**ATTENDANT**

Yet she is great and proud and known among all men.

**HIPPOLYTUS**

I do not care for gods men worship in the night.

**ATTENDANT**

Still you must recognise the honours due to gods.

**HIPPOLYTUS**

Both among gods and men there are different tastes.

**ATTENDANT**

Then I wish you happiness, and the sense you ought to have.

15

HIPPOLYTUS [*turning away from him*]
Come on, my friends, and go inside the house and see
the banquet is prepared. After a day of hunting
a well-spread table does one good. Let someone rub
the horses down. When I have had enough to eat,
I shall yoke and drive them out today for exercise.
As for your Cyprian goddess—may she be in luck.

[*He goes into the palace. The Attendant remains behind and bows before
the statue of Aphrodite.*]

ATTENDANT
But I (and here I shall not imitate young men)
think in a way a slave should think before he speaks.
Let me address my prayers to your holy image,
goddess of Cyprus. You should have some pity on
one who, because of his youth, with violent feelings
speaks nonsense of you. You should pretend not to hear.
Gods should be wiser and more moderate than men.

[*He follows the others into the palace. Enter the Chorus of Women of
Troezen.*]

CHORUS
There is a rock that wells with Ocean's water
and from its steeps lets fall a flowing stream
where pitchers dip, and there
one that I knew was plunging
red robes in the river dew,
spreading the robes to dry on the slab of a hot
rock in the sun, and she
told me first of the queen.

How she is wasting on a bed of sickness

16

inside her house, and hides her golden head
in the shade of a silken veil;
and now for the third day she
refrains with her lovely lips
from the touch of the grains of Demaeter, and secretly
suffering, longs to draw in
to the pitiful harbour of death.

Are you astray, my lady,
possessed by a god—by Pan
or Hecate or the terrible
Corybantes, or Mountain Mother?
Or are you wasted away for a sin incurred
by failing, unsanctified, to sacrifice
to the goddess of beasts, Dictynna?
For she is able to range through the waves
over the ocean to land
on the salt and eddying waters.

Is it your husband, the noble
king of Erectheus' sons?
Is he folded in secret love
away from your bed in the house?
Or has some mariner sailed from the port of Crete
to this most kindly harbour for sailing men
and brought to our queen a message?
And is it in grief for what she has learnt
of suffering there in her home
that she lies heartsick in her bed?

In women's difficult unstable natures
a pitiful helplessness often dwells
springing from pangs in the womb and unbalanced thought.
Such an impulse of pain

through my loins also has darted, but then I cried
to heavenly Artemis, giver of gentle birth,
goddess guarding the bow, and she for ever
is honoured and blessed by me as she goes with the gods.

[*Enter Phaedra and her old Nurse. Phaedra lies down on a couch.*]

But here at the door is the aged nurse
bringing her mistress out of the palace.
The lowering cloud on her brows is darker.
What can it be? I long to discover
what can have happened
so to alter the form of the queen.

NURSE

How people suffer! How hateful is illness!
What shall I do for you? What leave undone?
Here is the light for you, here is the bright sky.
Here is your sick bed ready for you
outside your doors.
What you wanted was always to come here,
though soon you will hurry back to your bedroom,
soon disappointed. Nothing can please you.
Discontented with what you have, you
think what you don't have is better.
I would rather be ill than look after an illness.
Illness is simple, but nursing an illness brings
grief to the heart and work for the hands.
The life of men is nothing but evil,
nor is there any respite from suffering.
Yet if there is a state better than living,
darkness surrounds it and hides it in clouds.
So we show ourselves lovesick indeed
for this something that glitters on earth,

having no knowledge of different living
and no revelation of what is beneath,
since there's no direction in idle legends.

PHAEDRA

Lift me upright, give support to my head.
Dear women, the bonds of my limbs are unloosed.
Take hold of my hands and my delicate arms.
Heavy to wear is the veil on my head.
Take it, and let my hair loose on my shoulders.

NURSE

Be patient, my child, and do not so fiercely
toss to and fro.
If you keep quiet and are brave in your spirit,
you will find your illness more easy to bear.
It is fated for mortals to suffer.

PHAEDRA

Alas! how I wish I could draw from a dewy
fountain a draught of the shining waters,
and take my rest in a leafy meadow,
lying beneath the shade of the poplars.

NURSE

O my child, what is this you are saying?
Really, you must not before all these people
speak and let loose such words ridden by madness.

PHAEDRA

Away to the mountains! I will go to the wild wood,
under the pines, where the hounds are hunting,
and pressing their chase on the dappled deer.
O, let me do it! I long to be shouting

out to the hounds, and to poise by my yellow
hair the Thessalian javelin, and carry
the bladed lance in my hand.

NURSE

My child, why ever should such things upset you?
Why should you take such an interest in hunting?
Why should you long for a draught from a fountain?
Here, close by your towers, is a dewy slope,
and from here we can fetch you some water.

PHAEDRA

Artemis, queen of sea-girt Limne,
queen of the race-course that echoes with hoof-beats,
O how I long to be there in your lowlands,
breaking in the Venetian horses!

NURSE

What are these words that you fling out in madness?
Only just now you were off to the mountains,
led by a longing for hunting, and now you
yearn for horses on sandy plains
away from the sea. It would take some divining
to find, my child, which one of the gods
holds the reins of your spirit, and drives it astray.

PHAEDRA

What can I have done to make me unhappy?
And whither so driven aside from my right mind?
I am mad, I have fallen through spite of some god,
O, poor wretch that I am.
Cover my face again, dear mother.
I feel dread at the words I have spoken.
Cover it up. Tears start in my eyes,

and shame has come over my face.
To come to my senses again in an agony;
yet this madness is evil. The best thing of all
is to die, and not know what I'm doing.

#### NURSE

There, I've covered your face. But, O when will my body
be shrouded in death?
Much I have learned by living a long time.
Mortals, I know, should join with each other
in loving feelings that are not excessive,
just on the surface, not touching the quick of the soul.
Light should the heart's affections lie on us,
quick to cast off and quick to pull tighter.
This is a heavy weight, that one soul
should suffer itself for two souls,
just as I for my mistress grieve too greatly.
In life, they say, one finds more failure
than delight in this unswerving
heart's devotion, which conflicts with health.
'Nothing in excess' is better
far than counsels of perfection.
Wise men will agree with me.

#### CHORUS

You aged woman, trusted nurse to this our queen.
We see the unhappy sufferings that Phaedra feels,
but what the illness is is still unknown to us.
From you we wish to hear and be informed of it.

#### NURSE

I have asked and do not know. She does not wish to speak.

#### CHORUS

Nor what was the beginning of these pains of hers?

NURSE

Just the same thing. On all of this she is silent.

CHORUS

How weak she is, and how her body wastes away!

NURSE

No wonder, since for three days she has touched no food.

CHORUS

Is it some curse of god or that she aims to die?

NURSE

She wants to die, and starves to make an end of life.

CHORUS

It is a strange thing if her husband bears this calmly.

NURSE

She hides her pains from him and says she is not ill.

CHORUS

But when he sees her face, does he not see she is?

NURSE

No. Just now he happens to be away from home.

CHORUS

Can you not try and force some way of finding out
What is her illness and what distraction of her mind?

NURSE

I have tried everything and met with no success.
But even now I'll not relax my efforts for her,

so that you too, being here, may bear me witness
how true I am to a mistress in her misfortune.

[*She turns to Phaedra.*]

Come, my dear child, and let us both forget those words
we spoke before. You must behave with more kindness,
relax that angry frown and change your way of mind;
and I, if in any way I failed to understand,
will let that be, and turn to other better words.
Now, if your illness is the kind that one keeps private,
here are these women ready to assist you in it.
But if your suffering can be disclosed to men,
speak, so that we can let the doctors know of it.
Now, come! Why don't you speak? You ought to tell me, child.
If what I say is not right, point it out to me;
otherwise you should agree with my well-meant advice.
Say something, do. Or look at me.—Poor wretch I am!
Women, it does no good, the trouble that we take.
We are still as far away as ever. The last time
words could not soften her, and now she will not hear.

[*She turns to Phaedra again.*]

Yet listen to this. Now, if you like, be more self-willed
than is the sea itself. Dying, you will betray
your children, leaving them without their share in all
their father's wealth. Yes, she, the Amazon huntress,
the royal lady, bore a master for your sons,
a bastard aiming at full rights. You know him well.
Hippolytus.

PHAEDRA
Alas!

23

NURSE

What! This point touches you?


PHAEDRA

Mother, you have destroyed me. Please, I beg of you,
never again make mention of this man to me.


NURSE

You see? Your mind is sound, and yet in spite of that
you will not help your children and preserve your life.


PHAEDRA

I love my children. Other evils storm my heart.


NURSE

Are your hands pure, my child, from stain of shedding blood?


PHAEDRA

My hands are pure: it is my mind that has the stain.


NURSE

Some enemy brings pain on you by magic means.


PHAEDRA

Against his will and mine a friend is killing me.


NURSE

Is it Theseus who has done some injury to you?


PHAEDRA

Let me be never found to have done him a wrong!


NURSE

What is this fearful thing that drives you on to death?

24

PHAEDRA

Leave me to sin. It is not against you I sin.


NURSE

I'll never leave you. It is your fault if I fail.


[*She throws herself on her knees in front of Phaedra.*]


PHAEDRA

What are you doing, clinging to my hands and forcing me?


NURSE

Yes, and I clasp your knees and will not let you go.


PHAEDRA

Poor thing, my words are bad for you to hear, yes, bad.


NURSE

Could anything be worse for me than to lose you?


PHAEDRA

You will be lost. And yet to me this thing gives fame.


NURSE

Yet you hide something good, in spite of all my prayers?


PHAEDRA

Yes, since the glory that I plan proceeds from shame.


NURSE

Then you will be more honoured still by telling it.


PHAEDRA

Leave me, I beg you, and let go of my right hand.

25

NURSE

Never! You will not give me what you ought to give.


PHAEDRA

I will. For I respect your rights in pleading so.


NURSE

Then I'll be silent. Now it is for you to speak.


PHAEDRA

O my mother, what a love, poor thing, you fell into!


NURSE

Is what you mean, my child, her passion for the bull?


PHAEDRA

You too, my wretched sister, Dionysus' wife.


NURSE

What is it, child? You speak ill of your family.


PHAEDRA

And I, the third unhappy one, I too destroyed!


NURSE

I am indeed bewildered. Where will these words end?


PHAEDRA

Where I became unhappy, a long time ago.


NURSE

But still I know no more of what I wish to hear.


PHAEDRA

Ah!
I wish that you could say the words I have to say.

NURSE

I am no prophetess to make the dark things clear.

PHAEDRA

What do they mean when they say people are in love?

NURSE

Something most sweet, my child, and also painful too.

PHAEDRA

I must be one who feels the painfulness of it.

NURSE

What's this you say? You are in love, my child?
With whom?

PHAEDRA

There is a man I know, the son of the Amazon . . .

NURSE

Hippolytus?

PHAEDRA

You heard it from your lips, not mine.

NURSE

Ah, child, what can you mean? O, you have ruined me.
Women, this is not to be borne, and I will not
bear to live more. Ill day, ill light it is I see.
I shall throw and cast away my body, leave my life
and die. I say farewell, since I no longer am.
Against their will, perhaps, but all the same, the wise
and chaste love evil. Cypris, then, is not divine,

27

but must be something else more mighty than a god
to have destroyed my mistress, me, and all our house.

Oh, did you hear her? Oh, did you listen
to things unutterable, to the queen
as she told her woes?
O let me die, dear lady, before
I come to a mind like yours! Oh alas!
O poor wretch in your pains!
O troubles in which men live!
You are destroyed, you have brought bad things to the light.
What waits for you now through this long day?
Some new evil will fall on this house.
No longer doubtful the destination
of Cypris' will, O unhappy daughter of Crete.

PHAEDRA
You women of Troizen, you who live here upon
this verge and entrance to the country of Pelops,
before now idly in the watches of the night
I have considered how the life of man is spoilt.
And to my mind it is not through a lack of wit
that men go wrong, since, as for being sensible,
many are that. But this is how I look at it:
we understand and recognise what things are good,
but do not do them, some because of laziness,
others by choosing pleasure of some kind instead
of honour. There are many pleasures in our life,—
long conversations, being idle (a delightful fault),
and shame. There are two kinds of shame,—the one not bad,
the other a weight on houses. If they were marked out
clearly, the two would not be spelt in the same way.
Now, since it happens that I think as I have said,

28

the medicine does not exist by which I was
likely to change and fall back from this view of mine.
Now to you too I shall describe my way of thought.
When passion wounded me, I tried to find the way
by which I could bear it with most honour. I began
in this way,—to keep silent and conceal my pain.
There is no trusting in the tongue, which well enough
knows how to criticise the thoughts of other men,
yet on its own self oftenest brings suffering.
And then my second resolution was to bear
my folly nobly and by reason conquer it.
And, as a third resource, since by these means I failed
to subdue Cypris, I made up my mind to die;
and this (no one will question it) is the best plan.
For I would never wish my good deeds to be hid,
nor to have people watching me when I do ill.
The deed, I knew, was shameful and my own disease;
clearly I knew as well that I was a woman,
something that's loathed by all. My curses on the wife
who first began, by taking lovers, to bring shame
upon the marriage bed! It was from noble houses
this evil started to descend on womankind.
When what is shameful is condoned by noble people,
then certainly the lower class will think it good.
And then I hate the women who in words are chaste,
while hiding secretly their bold dishonest deeds.
O sea-born lady Cypris, how can these ones ever
look in the faces of their husbands and not fear
and tremble lest the darkness that has covered them
and rooms within their houses might not cry aloud?
This is the thing, my friends, that drives me to my death:
lest I be found to have brought shame on my husband
and on the children whom I bore. I want them free
to live and free to speak and prosperous to dwell

in glorious Athens, famous for their mother's sake.
Consciousness of a father's or a mother's sins
enslaves a man, however stout his heart may be.
And this alone, they say, to those who have it, can
be matched with life itself,—a good and upright mind.
Time, at some moment, must bring evil men to light,
holding to them, as to the face of some young girl,
a mirror up. May I be never seen with them!

Ah, how what's wise and chaste is honoured everywhere,
and among men it bears the fruit of good report!

My mistress, as you saw, just now the news of your
predicament filled me with sudden dreadful fear.
But now I think that I was silly. Among men
one's second thoughts are in a way the wiser ones.
To you nothing outrageous or unheard-of has
happened. It is the goddess' anger strikes at you.
You are in love. What's strange in that? Most people are.
And then because of love will you destroy your life?
There'll be no point in loving those who are close to us
now or in future, if one has to die for it.
Cypris is irresistible when in full force,
but gently visits those whose spirits yield to her;
and when she finds a man who's proud and arrogant,
of course she seizes him and makes a mock of him.
She ranges through the air, and in the surge of sea
there Cypris is, and everything proceeds from her.
And she it is who plants in us and gives desire
from which all we inhabitants of earth are born.
Indeed those people who possess the books of old

30

writers and are themselves great readers of their works
know how Zeus once desired to have the joys of love
with Semele, and know how once fair-shining Dawn
snatched up to heaven Cephalus to join the gods,
and all this out of passion; and yet, all the same,
they dwell in heaven, do not shun the paths of gods,
and are, I think, quite pleased to yield to what has passed.
Will you object? Your father then should have made you
on special terms, or else controlled by other gods,
if you will not consent to follow these known laws.
How many men, and wise ones, are there, do you think,
who see their beds defiled, and pretend not to see?
How many fathers who assist their erring sons
in finding love affairs? Amongst the wise this is
a general rule,—to hide what is not fair to see.
Nor should men try to be too strict about their lives.
They cannot even make the roofs, with which their homes
are covered, absolutely right. And you, fallen
to such a state, how can you hope to swim out clear?
No, if the good in you is greater than the bad,
you, being only human, will do very well.
So, please, my dear child, give up these bad thoughts of yours.
Give up your arrogance, for it is nothing else
but arrogance to wish to have more strength than gods.
Love, and be bold. It is a god that willed all this.
You may be ill, but find a way to come out well.
Charms do exist and words that soothe and sway the mind.
We shall discover medicine for this ill of yours.
Indeed it's true that men would still be looking for it,
unless it was we women could find out the way.

CHORUS

Phaedra, she tells you things that are more useful to you
in your present distress. Yet I think *you* are right.

31

And you will find this view of mine more hard to bear
than are her words, more painful too to listen to.

PHAEDRA

This is the thing that ruins the well-ordered towns
and homes of men,—words spoken too persuasively.
For people should not say what charms the listener's ear
but what will bring to those who hear it good report.

NURSE

Why this grand language? What you need is not fine words
but to find out as fast as possible about
the man, and us to tell him the straight story of you.
For if it was not that your life was in this state
of peril, if you were a woman more controlled,
I never would, because of love and your delights,
have urged you on so far; but now the struggle is
to save your life, and I cannot be blamed for this.

PHAEDRA

What awful things you say! Will you please keep your mouth
shut, and never again speak such disgraceful words.

NURSE

Disgraceful, yes, but better for you than your fine
words, and a better deed if I can save your life
than save your name, to glory in which name you'd die.

PHAEDRA

Please, not to me, I beg you (you speak well, but foully)
go any further now. My heart is well prepared
by love, and, if you speak so well of shameful things,
I shall be swept away by what I fly from now.

**NURSE**

If this is what you think, you ought not to have sinned.
You have. Then listen to me, for the next best thing
is to give way. I have at home some soothing draughts
for love,—the thought has only just occurred to me,—
and these, without dishonour, doing no harm to your wits,
will free you from your sickness, if you will be brave.
But I must have something from him whom you desire,
some mark, either a lock of hair or piece of clothing,
so from the two of you to make consentment one.

**PHAEDRA**

Is this a drug to drink or ointment to put on?

**NURSE**

I do not know. Be happy and never mind, my child.

**PHAEDRA**

I am afraid that you may be too clever in all this.

**NURSE**

Be sure you would fear everything. What do you fear?

**PHAEDRA**

That you might tell some word of this to Theseus' son.

**NURSE**

Leave me alone, my child. I shall arrange things well.

[*She turns to go into the palace but first addresses the statue of Aphrodite.*]

Only be you my helper, lady of the sea,

C                    33

Cypris! As for what else I have within my mind
it will be enough to tell it to our friends indoors.

[*She goes into the palace.*]

Love, O Love, you that make well to the eyes
drops of desire, you that bring sweet delight
into the hearts that you with your force invade,
never to me appear in catastrophe,
never in discord come!
Since there exists no bolt of the fire and no
weightier bolt of the stars than that
arrow of Aphrodite hurled
out of the hands of Love,
Love, the child of the Highest.


Useless it is that still by Alpheus' stream,
Useless it is by Phoebus's Pythian shrines
for the land of Hellas to sacrifice more and more
blood of oxen, when we neglect to give
the honour that's due to Love,
Love, the ruler of men, he who keeps the keys
of Aphrodite's pleasantest dwelling-place,
he who ravages on his way,
bringing to mortals all
catastrophes at his coming.


The girl in Oichalia,
a maiden unyoked to love,
unmarried as yet and husbandless Cypris took
and loosed her from home in ships,
and, a fugitive thing, like a nymph or Bacchante, she gave her,

34

with blood and with fire
and murder for wedding hymns,
to Alcimene's child.
Poor wretch she was in her marriage!

O holy fortress of Thebes,
O fountain of Dirce, you
well could witness the force of Cypris' coming.
For with thunder and lightning flash
she brought to her bed the mother of Bacchus, the Zeus-born,
and gave her a wedding
with death for a fate. She breathes
in terror on all
and flies on her way like a bee.

[*Phaedra goes to the door of the palace and listens.*]

PHAEDRA

Be silent, women! O now, I am really ruined!

CHORUS

What is it, Phaedra, frightens you inside your house?

PHAEDRA

Be quiet. Let me hear the voice of those inside.

CHORUS

I will. Though this beginning seems to me not good.

PHAEDRA

Oh! Oh! alas! alas!
O wretched thing I am in these my sufferings!

35

### CHORUS

What are the words you speak? What is the tale you tell?
Say what speech it is, my lady, that frightens you so,
tearing into your heart.

### PHAEDRA

O I am lost! Just stand beside these gates, and there
listen to all the uproar falling on the house.

### CHORUS

You are there by the door. You it is who must tell
of the words that come from within.
Tell me what can it be, what evil is here.

### PHAEDRA

He shouts aloud, the son of the huntress Amazon,
Hippolytus, and to my nurse says dreadful things.

### CHORUS

Yes, I can hear the voice; yet cannot clearly tell
whence came the cry to you,
came to you through the gates.

### PHAEDRA

O listen, clearly now he calls her 'procuress
of evil and betrayer of her master's bed.'

### CHORUS

O, I weep for your pain. Lady, you are betrayed.
How can I find you help?
Secret things are revealed, and you are lost . . .

### PHAEDRA

Alas! Alas!

36

By your friends betrayed.


PHAEDRA

She has destroyed me, telling him of my distress,
kindly, not nobly, seeking to relieve my pain.


CHORUS

What now? What will you do, caught so much in a trap?


PHAEDRA

I do not know, except for one thing,—that quick death
remains the only cure for all my present pain.

[*Phaedra retires. Hippolytus, with the Nurse following him, comes in.*]


HIPPOLYTUS

O mother Earth and you unfoldings of the sun,
I have heard the unspeakable sound of most foul words.


NURSE

Be silent, child, lest someone notices your cries.


HIPPOLYTUS

I have heard dreadful things. How can I hold my tongue?


NURSE

I beg you, by this right hand of yours, and this strong arm.


HIPPOLYTUS

Take your hands off me! Do not dare to touch my clothes.


NURSE

I implore you by your knees. Do not be my ruin.

37

## HIPPOLYTUS

How can I, if, as you pretend, your words were good?

## NURSE

O child, this story is not fit for all to hear.

## HIPPOLYTUS

More hearers the more honour, when the news is good.

## NURSE

O child, you must respect the oath you swore to me.

## HIPPOLYTUS

It was my tongue that swore: my mind has made no oath.

## NURSE

O child, what will you do? Will you destroy your friends?

## HIPPOLYTUS

Your words revolt me. No bad person is my friend.

## NURSE

Have pity! It is natural, my child, to make mistakes.

## HIPPOLYTUS

O Zeus, why did you house them in the light of day,
women, man's evil, a false glittering counterfeit?
For if you wished to propagate the race of men,
this should not have been brought about by women's means.
Instead men should have offered in exchange their wealth
within your temples,—gold or silver or a weight
of bronze,—and bought their children for the price they paid,
each at its proper value. And then they could live
in free and easy homes and have no need of wives.

This makes it clear how great an evil a woman is:
the father who breeds and educates one pays a dowry too
that she may live elsewhere and he be free from pain.
And then the man who takes this curse inside his house
delights in adding fine adornments to her shape,
worthless itself, spends time in finding dresses for her,
the fool, and wastes away the substance of his house.
He's in a cleft stick; for, if he can marry well
and likes his new relations, then his wife will be
a bitter thing; and, if his wife is good, he'll find
worthless relations, bad and good luck counterpoised.
Easiest for him who has settled in his home a wife
whose mind's a total blank, a simple useless thing.
I hate a clever woman, and in my house never would
have one with more ideas than women ought to have.
For Cypris inculcates more often evil ways
among the clever ones, whereas the helpless kind
are barred from loose behaviour by their lack of wit.
No servant ever should have access to a wife:
their company should be some biting speechless beast,
so that they could not even speak to anyone,
nor get an answer back from those whom they address.
But as it is wives who are bad make their bad plots
at home, and then their servants carry them outside.
Like you, you miserable wretch, who came to me
to make arrangements for my father's sacred bed.
With running water I shall wash my ears and wipe
away your words. How could I ever be so base,
I, who, just hearing you, must think myself unclean?
Be sure what saves you, woman, is my sense of right.
If, carelessly, I had not bound myself by oaths,
for sure I should have told my father of all this.
And now, so long as Theseus is away from home,
I shall be absent too, and keep a silent tongue;

39

and then, returning with my father, I shall watch
how you will meet his eye, you and your mistress too.
Yes, I shall know, having tasted of your shamelessness.
I would destroy you all,—never shall have enough
of hating women, though they say that I'm always
saying the same thing. Women too are always bad.
Either let someone teach them to be self-controlled
or else allow me still to tread them under foot.

[*Hippolytus goes out. Phaedra comes forward.*]

PHAEDRA

O sad they are, unlucky,
the fates that women have!
Now that our hopes are betrayed, what art
What words can we find to loose the knot of his speech?
The verdict is given. O earth, and light!
Where can I go to escape my fate?
How, dear friends, can I hide my pain?
Which of the gods would succour me now? What man
can appear to stand beside me as fellow worker
in evil deeds? O no, my life's disaster
stays with me still and cannot be escaped.
I am the most unlucky one of women.

CHORUS

Alas! it is all over. They miscarried, those
arts of your servant, lady. Things are bad indeed.

PHAEDRA [*to the Nurse*]

You wicked woman, you destroyer of your friends,
what have you done to me? I pray my parent Zeus
may blot you out entirely with a blow of fire!
Did I not tell you, seeing in advance your mind,

40

to make no mention of what now has brought me shame?
But you had no restraint, and now no longer can I die
with a good name. I greatly need some new device.
Hippolytus, with anger sharpening his mind,
will speak against me, tell his father of your sins,
and tell the aged Pittheus of my sufferings,
and fill the whole land with the shameful story of it.
My curse on you, and on all those who are so keen
to help friends in dishonest ways against their will!

NURSE

You, lady, can reproach me for the wrong I did;
the hurt you feel is stronger than your power to judge.
Yet I too can reply to this, if you will hear.
I brought you up and seek your good. I tried to find
medicine for your disease, and found not what I wished.
Had I been lucky, I should have been thought most wise
since brains are measured by the way events fall out.

PHAEDRA

Is this your sense of right and proper speech to me,—
to wound me first, and then admit as much in words?

NURSE

Our speeches are too long. I have been indiscreet.
Yet from all this, my child, there is a safe way out.

PHAEDRA

Stop talking. You have given me before advice
that was dishonest, and your action too was bad.
So now begone out of my sight, think of yourself;
and I shall act with honour in my own affairs.
And now I ask you, noble daughters of Troizen,
to listen to my prayers and grant me this request,—
to hide in silence all that you have heard of here.

**CHORUS**

I swear by mighty Artemis, the child of Zeus,
not ever to bring any of your woes to light.

**PHAEDRA**

You have spoken fairly. Now, searching my mind, I find
one way and one alone to meet my present pass,
so as to leave my children honour in their lives
and help myself in what has happened to me now.
For I shall never put my Cretan home to shame
or, after these disgraceful doings, come within
the sight of Theseus, just to save one single life.

**CHORUS**

What evil without cure do you intend to do?

**PHAEDRA**

To die; but how to die is what I now shall plan.

**CHORUS**

O do not say such words!

**PHAEDRA**

You must give good advice.
In parting from my life upon this very day
I shall give joy to Cypris who is destroying me.
Bitter has been the love which brings me my defeat,
yet I, in death, shall prove at least an evil thing
to another, so that he may learn not to be proud
in my misfortune. He will have a share with me
in this complaint of mine, and so learn modest ways.

*[Phaedra goes into the palace.]*

O I would be in aerial hiding-places,
that a god might set me there in the flying flocks,
myself a bird on the wing!
I would be borne on high
to the waves of the sea on the Adriatic shore,
to Eridanus' waters, where
into the dark-blue stream,
pitying Phaethon, the luckless Heliades
melt in their bright and amber-shining tears.

Or might I make my way to the apple gardens
of the singing Hesperides, where the dark sea's lord
ends the journeys of ships!
There he dwells in the terrible
verge of heaven that Atlas holds with his arms,
and ambrosial fountains flow
from the resting places of Zeus,
from his palace halls where life-giving holy earth
still for the gods increases their happiness.

White-winged vessel from Crete
that, through the salt of the wave and the beat of the sea
bore my mistress away from her happy home
with a prize of unfortunate love!
Surely ill-starred both ways, or at least from Crete,
to famous Athens it winged its way,
and there on Munichian shores
they tied the ends of their twisted ropes
and set their feet on the land.

For that Aphrodite broke
her heart with the terrible sickness of passion impure.
Now, since she is overladen with hard events,
she will tie to her bridal roof

43

the hanging noose of a rope, and fit it tight
to the white of her neck, being filled with shame
at the face of the hateful goddess.
First she will choose good fame and to rid
her heart of the pains of love.

[A Servant is heard crying out inside the palace.]

SERVANT

Oh! Oh!
Come here and help, all you that are about the house!
Our mistress and the wife of Theseus is hanged.

CHORUS

Alas! Alas! It is all over, now no more
the royal lady lives, hanged in the swinging noose.

SERVANT

Be quick! Let someone bring a knife with double edge
with which we can unloose the knot about her neck.

CHORUS

What should we do, my friends? Do you think we should go
inside and loose our lady from the choking rope?

SEMI-CHORUS

Why should we? Are there not young men as servants there?
By being over-zealous we may risk our lives.

SERVANT

Set the limbs straight, and so lay out this wretched body.
Sad for my master is this housekeeping of hers.

CHORUS

Now she is dead, I hear it, this unhappy woman.
Already they lay out her body as a corpse.

[Enter Theseus with his attendants. Since he has been on some religious
journey, he is wearing a garland on his head.]

44

Do you know, women, what this uproar means indoors?
A noise of wailing from my servants reached my ears.
Strange that they do not think it right to unbar the gates
and kindly greet me back from my religious way.
Surely no ill has happened to aged Pittheus?
He is already far advanced in life, yet still,
were he to leave us, it would be a grief to me.

Theseus, this is a thing that does not touch the old.
It is the death of youth that will bring pain to you.

Alas! Not that my children's life is stolen away?

They live. Their mother,—sad, most sad for you—is dead.

What do you say? My wife dead? How then did she die?

She fastened up a running noose to hang herself.

Had grief frozen her blood, or did some evil come to her?

So much I know, no more. I too have only just,
Theseus, approached your house in mourning for your loss.

Ah, why then have I set this crown of woven leaves

45

upon my head, unlucky in my holy voyage?
Come, men, undo the bolts that bar the double doors!
Loosen the chains, that I may see this bitter sight
of my dead wife who, by her death, has destroyed me.

[*The doors are opened and the body of Phaedra is discovered.*]

CHORUS
Oh, alas, poor lady, your pitiful fate!
You have suffered and done
a deed that can utterly ruin this house.
O reckless your doing, this violent death
in the sinful event, overthrown,
O pitiful, by your own hand!
Which god, my poor lady, has taken the light from your life?

THESEUS
O I weep for my pain! O my city, this is
the worst of the things I have suffered. O fate,
how heavy have you fallen on me and my house,
a spreading stain unknown from some avenging power,
or rather a murderer's blow taking the life from my life.
And an ocean of evil, poor wretch, is in front of my eyes
so great that I can never more swim clear of it
nor cross beyond the wave of this catastrophe.
Alas! my wife, what word can I find,
how can I name your burden of fate?
For like a bird you slipped out of the hand away
from me and leaped a sheer leap to the house of death.
O how pitiful is this suffering! O, alas!
Out of the past somewhere I am reaping the fate
sent by a god for the sins
of someone who lived of old.

46

My lord, these evils have not come to you alone.
You have lost a worthy wife, and so have many more.

THESEUS

Below the earth, in the cloud that's below the earth
I wish to dwell in the dark, I wish to die,
now separated from your dear companionship;
for, perishing, you have destroyed more than yourself.
O, what news can I hear? Whence, poor wife, did it come,
the fate of death to your heart?
Can someone tell me what was done? Or does my royal house
uselessly shelter numbers of my serving men?
O, my heart aches for you!
O I pity the grief I have seen in my home
It is not to be borne and not to be told. I am lost.
My home is empty and my children motherless.
You have left me, left me behind,
dearest of women and best that the ray of the sun
sees, or the star-faced moon in the night.

CHORUS

Alas, unhappy, the pain that fills the house!
Streaming with tears my eyes
melt for your fate. And for long
I tremble at the woe that will come next.

THESEUS

Ha!
What can this mean, this letter that is hanging down
from her dear hand? Has she some news she wants to tell?
Surely she has written down, poor thing, her will about
the children and my love, and made me some request.
Poor creature, be at rest! No woman in the world

47

will enter Theseus' bed or come within his house.
And now the prints of that gold signet ring she had,
she who no longer lives,—these seem to touch my heart.
Come, let me break the fastenings about the seals
and see what thing it is this letter wants to say.

CHORUS

Alas! Alas! Here now a god brings on
evil news in its turn. To me no fate
of life deserves to be lived after this that is done.
For I speak of our master's home, alas, alas,
as being destroyed, as being a thing of the past.
O god, if such there be, do not betray this house
but listen to my prayer; for, like a prophetess,
from omens I can see the evil on its way.

THESEUS

O what a fearful wrong upon the top of wrong!
Unspeakable, insufferable, O alas!

CHORUS

What is it? Speak if I may share the news at all.

THESEUS

This letter cries and cries what cannot be forgot.
Where can I leave my weight of woe? O, I am lost indeed,
utterly lost! What a speaking strain
in her writing I saw! Ah me!

CHORUS

Alas, the word you speak leads on the way to pain.

THESEUS

I can keep it no longer behind the gates of my lips,

48

this evil so deadly, so hard to be mended.
Oh, my city!
Hippolytus has dared to violate my bed
by force and shown contempt for Zeus's holy eye.
O now Poseidon, father, you who promised me
the power to curse three times, with one of these do you
destroy my son, and let him not survive this day.
Do this, if you indeed gave me the power to curse.

CHORUS

My lord, recall that curse, I beg you, back again.
Soon you will see that you were wrong. O listen to me!

THESEUS

It is impossible. And also I shall drive
him from this land. By one or other fate he will
be crushed. Either Poseidon, honouring my curse,
will end his life and send him to the gates of Hell,
or else, in exile from this land and wandering
abroad, he will live through a hard and bitter life.

[*Enter Hippolytus with his attendants.*]

CHORUS

Look, here Hippolytus, your son, has come himself
at the right time. Relax your cruel anger, lord
Theseus, and make the best decision for your house.

HIPPOLYTUS

I heard your cry, my father, and have come to you
with all speed. Yet I do not know what thing it is
for which you grieve. This I would like to learn from you.
O, what is this? My father, now I see your wife

D                              49

lying dead there. This is a thing to wonder at.
She whom only just now I parted from, she who
not long ago was looking on the light of day!
What happened to her? In what way was she destroyed?
Father, it is from you I wish to learn of this.
You do not speak? Yet silence does no good in pain;
for, when the heart desires to hear of everything,
it must in trouble also be inquisitive.
Then, father, surely it cannot be right to hide
your misery from friends and even more than friends.

THESEUS

O how men uselessly and often go astray!
Why give instruction in the many countless arts,
use all devices, make inventions of all kinds,
while one thing is not known and never studied yet—
to teach intelligence to those who have no sense?

HIPPOLYTUS

Some clever expert you must mean, who has the power
to force to wisdom those who are deprived of it.
But, father, this is not the time for sophistry.
I fear your sufferings must have deranged your speech.

THESEUS

Alas! there should have been for men some certain sign
to mark their friends, some way of reading in their minds
which one is true and which one not a friend at all;
everyone should have had two different tones of voice,
one for his plain just dealings, one for all the rest.
Then words from false minds could have been compared and
judged
by what was true, and I should not have been deceived.

No, surely none of my friends has spoken ill of me
into your ear? And, innocent, am I diseased?
Sir, I am all amazed, and what amazes me
is your strange words that seem to leave the path of sense.

O mind of man! To what lengths will it not proceed?
Where will a bound be set to reckless arrogance?
For if in every generation this swells up,
if the younger comes to an excess of shame beyond
the former generation, then the gods will have
to add another world to this one, which will hold
the evil men who are by nature all depraved.
Look at this young man here, who, though he is my son,
has brought pollution to my bed, and without doubt
is proved the greatest villain by this woman's death.
And now, since any way your presence stains the air,
turn your head here, and let your father see your face.
So you are he who, as a man marked out, consorts
with gods? You are the chaste one, all untouched by sin?
I certainly will not believe your boasting words
or be a fool to credit gods with ignorance.
Now boast away, try to impose on people with
your meatless meals, take Orpheus for your lord and join
the revel, worshipping the smoke of countless books.
You are found out. And people of your sort I bid
all men avoid. You are of those who seek their prey
by pompous language while you scheme your shameful deeds.
She's dead. And do you think that this will make you safe?
No, you mean creature. This is where you are most caught.
For where will you find oaths, where words to be more strong
for your acquittal than this argument of her?
You will pretend she hated you, and say bastards

and true-born children are by nature enemies.
That would suggest she bargained badly with her life,
through hating you to throw away what she loved best.
Or will you say that folly does not go with men
but is a part of woman's nature? I know well
young men no more reliable than women are
when Cypris brings confusion to their youthful hearts,
although they have advantages by being men.
But why should I thus meet you in a strife of words,
When this dead body here is surest evidence?
Go! Leave this land, an exile, quick as you can do,
and neither enter god-built Athens nor the bounds
of any country over which my spear holds sway.
I have suffered from you, and if I am worsted by you,
then Sinis of the Isthmus can deny the fact
I ever killed him, say it was an empty boast,
and Sciron's rocks that fall into the sea can say
I am not heavy on the doers of bad deeds.

CHORUS

How can I say that anyone at all of men
is happy? What was first is overturned again.

HIPPOLYTUS

Father, the rage and tension in your heart make me
afraid. As for the charge, there are good arguments,
yet, when examined, then it is not fair at all
I have no skill at making speeches to a crowd
and am wiser with a few who are my own equals.
This too is natural. Those who among the wise
are fools show more intelligence in speaking to
a crowd. Yet, all the same, since I am in this pass,
I am bound to loose my tongue. And I shall start my speech
from where you first attacked me surreptitiously,

thinking to injure me and give me no reply.
You see this light and earth. In them there is not one,
deny it as you may, who is more pure than I.
For, first, I know how to give reverence to the gods
and to have friends who will not try to injure me,
whose sense of shame prevents them asking what is bad
or aiding their associates in wicked deeds.
I, father, do not mock at those with whom I live,
but, near or far, am still a friend in the same way.
One thing has never touched me,—what you think my guilt.
This body to this moment is unstained by love.
I do not know the action, except what I hear
in talk or see in pictures, and I have no wish
to know about such things. I have a virgin soul.
Perhaps my purity does not convince your mind.
Then you must show in what way I became corrupt.
Was it this woman's body was more beautiful
than that of all the rest? Or did I hope to make
your house my own by taking on an heiress' bed?
Could I be such a fool, so quite outside my mind?
Or do wise-minded men enjoy the sweets of power?
They do not. For, when power is absolute, it will
always corrupt the minds of men who feel its charm.
For me, I'd choose to win in the Hellenic games
first prize, and in my city be the second man,
and so live happy always with my noble friends.
This means an active life with no danger attached,
and gives more pleasure than the life of supreme power.
    One thing in my defence I have not said. The rest
you know. But, if I had a witness like myself,
and if this woman saw the light when I was tried,
then, looking at the evidence, you would have seen
which was the guilty. Now, I swear to you by Zeus,
guardian of oaths, by earth's floor, that I never touched

your wife, nor could have wished to, nor conceived the thought.
And may I die inglorious, without a name,
without a house or city, exiled and wandering,
and, after death, let neither sea nor land receive
my body, if in truth I am a wicked man.
And, if it was from terror that she threw away
her life, I do not know. More than this I must not say.
She has controlled herself, though lacking in the power;
I have the power, but have made bitter use of it.

CHORUS

You have said enough to turn away the charge from you,
swearing an oath, no small conviction, to the gods.

THESEUS

Is he some wizard or enchanter who believes
that by his even temper he can get his way
over my spirit, after having wronged his sire?

HIPPOLYTUS

This too in you, my father, fills me with surprise.
If I had been your father and you been my son,
I should have killed you, not punished you with exile,
if you had dared to lay your hands upon my wife.

THESEUS

That is just like you. No, you shall not die like this,
according to the law you frame to suit yourself.
For a quick death is easiest for wicked men.
But, wandering in exile from your father's land,
abroad you will live through a hard and bitter life.
For this is the correct reward for wicked men.

HIPPOLYTUS

Alas! What will you do? Will you not wait for time
to inform against me? Will you drive me from the land?

**THESEUS**

Yes, and beyond the sea and bounds that Atlas made,
if I might do it, so I hate the sight of you.

**HIPPOLYTUS**

Will you not test the truth by oaths or guarantees
or words of seers, but banish me without a trial?

**THESEUS**

This letter here, with no prophetic stamp on it,
is evidence enough against you. As for birds
that flit above my head, I take no stock of that.

**HIPPOLYTUS**

O gods, why then can I not loose my lips,
I who by you am ruined, you whom I revere?
I cannot. Even then I'd fail to move the minds
I should move, and would vainly break the oath I swore.

**THESEUS**

Oh, these grand airs of yours will drive me to my grave!
Will you not go, and leave at once your father's house?

**HIPPOLYTUS**

O where then can I turn, poor wretch? Which of my friends
will take me to his house, exiled on such a charge?

**THESEUS**

One who enjoys receiving guests who will defile
other men's wives and take their share in deeds of shame.

**HIPPOLYTUS**

Ah! This goes to my heart and brings me near to tears,
that I should look so bad and you should think me so.

#### THESEUS

This time to groan and feel the future was the time
you dared commit an outrage on your father's wife.

#### HIPPOLYTUS

O palace, how I wish that you would cry aloud
for me, and witness whether I am really bad!

#### THESEUS

You wisely look for witnesses that have no voice.

[*He points to the dead body.*]

This fact that does not speak proclaims your wickedness.

Alas!
#### HIPPOLYTUS
I wish that I could stand in front of my own self
and see my face. I would have wept for what I feel.

#### THESEUS

Yes, you are much more trained in worshipping yourself
than in honouring your father with an honest mind.

#### HIPPOLYTUS

O my poor mother, bitter was your birth of me!
Let bastards never be among the friends I have!

#### THESEUS

Drag him out, slaves! Do you not hear? For long
I have been ordering this man to leave my land.

#### HIPPOLYTUS

The first of them who touches me will suffer for it.
Thrust me away yourself, if this is what you will.

56

THESEUS

That is what I shall do, if you will not obey.
No trace of pity for your exile touches me.

[*Exit Theseus.*]

HIPPOLYTUS

Then it is fixed, it seems. O, what a wretch I am!
I know the truth, but do not know how I can speak.
O child of Leto, dearest to me of the gods,
who rested with me, hunted with me, must I leave
great Athens as an exile? O farewell, you land
and city of Erechtheus! O, Troezenian plains,
what happiness you gave me as I grew up here!
Farewell! I see you for the last time as I speak.
Now come, my friends and young companions of this land,
speak to me now and see me on my way abroad.
Never will you behold a man more pure than I,
even although my father does not think it so.

[*Exit Hippolytus with his friends and attendants.*]

CHORUS

Greatly indeed it will ease me of grief, when it comes to my mind,
the thought of the gods.
Yet, though guessing in hope at their wisdom,
I am downcast again when I look at the fortunes and actions of
mortals,
for they alter, now here and now there;
man's life has no fixed station
but is mutable always.

I wish when I make my prayers this fate from the gods might be
mine—

57

to have wealth for my lot
and a heart unacquainted with grief.
And the thoughts in my mind should not be too subtle, nor
              counterfeit either;
but, easily willing to alter
my ways as the morrow comes,
I should always be happy.


No more can I look with a mind undisturbed upon things
              unexpected,
now the brightest of stars
of Hellas, of Athens,—we saw it—
is sent by the rage of his father
to foreign countries abroad.
O sands of the shores of my city,
O glades in the mountains where he
slew wild beasts with his swift-footed hounds,
and holy Dictynna was with him!


No more will you stand in the chariot drawn by Venetian fillies
on the Limnean track,
holding in with your foot the wild horses.
And the sleepless strain of the lyre
will cease in your father's house.
Unwreathed in the green of the forest
are the coverts of Leto's child.
In your exile the contest is ended
of maidens who vied for your love.


O for your misfortune I shall pass
in tears my ill-fated fate.
Useless, poor mother, was your birth of him.

My anger falls on the gods.
Alas, you band of the Graces,
why have you sent him away
from this house, from his native land,
he, quite without guilt in this evil?

[*A Messenger, one of Hippolytus' attendants approaches.*]

CHORUS

But now I see one of Hippolytus' men.
He comes up to the house in haste with a wild look.

MESSENGER

Women, which is the way for me to go to find
Theseus, this country's king? If you know where he is,
then tell me of it. Is he now inside the house?

CHORUS

I see him there coming himself outside the house.

MESSENGER

Theseus, I bring you tidings that will make you think,
you and your citizens that live in Athens' town
and in the boundaries of this Troizenian land.

THESEUS

What is it? Can it be that some fresh blow of fate
has come upon these twin and neighbouring towns of mine?

MESSENGER

Let me speak plain. Hippolytus no more exists.
He sees the light, but life is hanging by a thread.

59

Who killed him? Was it one who hated him because
his wife, like mine, was violated and defiled?

It was the chariot he drove that caused his death;
that, and the curses from your mouth which you called down
from the sea's governor, your father, on your son.

Gods! O Poseidon, so in very truth you were
my father, since you heard the prayer I made to you!
How did he die? Tell me. What was the way in which
the trap of Justice closed on him who shamed me so?

We were beside the promontory where the waves
beat on the shore, and combing down the horses' manes,
weeping, because a messenger had come to say
that now no longer must Hippolytus set foot
within this land, condemned by you to sad exile.
And then he came himself with the same strain of tears
to us upon the shore, and at his heels there came
with him a countless band of friends of his own age.
For long he did not cease lamenting. Then he said:
'Why do I rave? My father's words must be obeyed.
Prepare my yoke of horses for the chariot,
attendants. In this city I have no more right.'
And then each one of us pressed onward with the work,
and, quicker than it takes to tell, we had the mares
standing all ready harnessed in our master's sight.
Then from the chariot rail he snatches up the reins,
plants his feet firmly in the sockets on the floor,
and, stretching out his hands, he first addressed the gods:

'O Zeus, if I am sinful, let me cease to live,
and let my father know that he is wronging me
either when I am dead or while I see the light.'
And straight away he took into his hands the goad
and laid it on the horses, while we men ran on
close to the chariot's reins in escort to our lord,
on the straight road to Argos and Epidaurus.
Now, when we reached the open country just beyond
the frontier of this land, there is a stretch of shore
that lies already facing the Saronic gulf.
Here from the ground a roar like Zeus' thunderclap
came sounding heavy round us, terrible to hear.
The horses raised their heads and pricked their ears right up
into the air, and on us fell a lively fear,
wondering what the sound could be. And when we looked
along the foaming shores, we saw a monstrous wave
towering up to the sky, so big it took away
the view of Sciron's promontory from my eyes.
It hid the Isthmus and Asclepius' rock.
Next, swelling up and surging onward, with, all round,
a mass of foam, and with the roaring of the sea,
it neared the shore where stood the four-horse chariot.
And, in the very surge and breaking of the flood,
the wave threw up a bull, a fierce and monstrous thing,
and with his bellowing the land was wholly filled,
and fearfully re-echoed. As for us who saw
the sight, it seemed too much for eyes to look upon.
Immediately a dreadful panic seized the steeds.
My master, with his long experience of how
horses behave, gripped tightly in his hands the reins
and pulled upon them, like a boatman pulls his oar,
knotting the straps behind him and leaning back on them.
But the horses, taking in their teeth the fiery bits,
carried him on by force and took no care at all

either of master hand or of the knotted reins
or of the welded chariot; and, if he steered their course,
as with a tiller, to the smoother bits of ground,
then in their faces there appeared, to turn them back,
the bull, and drove the four-horse team all mad with fear.
And, if they rushed with maddened minds upon the rocks,
he silently drew near the chariot, and ran
alongside, till, forcing the wheel against a stone,
he overthrew the car and hurled the driver out.
Then all was huddled in a mass. The naves of wheels
and axle pins together flew into the air.
Hippolytus himself, entangled in the reins,
tied in inextricable bonds, was dragged along,
his dear head dashed upon the rocks, his flesh all torn,
and crying out words terrible for us to hear.
'O stop, you horses that were fed within my stalls!
Do not wipe out my life! Alas, my father's curse!
Will no one come to me and save a noble man?'
And many of us longed to do so, but we were
left far behind. Yet in the end he was set free
somehow or other from the bonds of these fine reins,
and fell down with a little life left in him still.
The horses and that awful monster of a bull
had disappeared somewhere along the rocky ground.
My lord, I am a slave within your house, and yet
this is a thing that I shall never be induced
to think,—that your son really was a wicked man:
no, not if all the race of women hung themselves,
or if all Ida's pines were filled with written words,
I'd not believe it, since I know that he is good.

CHORUS

Now the disaster of fresh evil is fulfilled.
From fate and from necessity there's no escape.

**THESEUS**

In hatred for the man who met this fate I was
pleased with your news. But now I feel a reverent awe
both towards the gods and him, since he was born of me;
and by these evils I am neither pleased nor grieved.

**MESSENGER**

What are we now to do to please you? Shall we bring
this suffering creature here, or what are we to do?
Think carefully. And my advice to you would be
not to be cruel to your own son in his pain.

**THESEUS**

Bring him to me, that I may see before my eyes
him who denied that he had made my bed his own,
that I by words and acts of gods may prove him wrong.

**CHORUS**

The unbending minds of gods and men,
Cypris, are prisoners to you,
and with you goes on wheeling swiftest wing
the gleaming feathered god.
He flies above the earth, above
the salt resounding sea.
Love brings enchantment when in shine of gold
and winged he comes upon the maddened heart.
He charms the tribes of mountain beasts,
beasts of the sea and all that earth supplies,
all creatures brightened by the seeing sun;
men too, and, Cypris, you alone
rule over all with sovereign power.

*[The goddess Artemis appears.]*

63

You I address and bid you to listen,
great son of Aigeus!
The daughter of Leto, I, Artemis speak to you.
Why are you foolishly pleased with this, Theseus,
you who have wickedly murdered your son,
led to believe by your wife's false words
uncertain things? You have gained certain ruin.
How you would wish in the depths of the earth
to hide your body in shame, or, changing
your life to the air, be a bird and keep far
away from this pain!
Since among good men there is certainly
no lot in life for you.
Hear, Theseus, now the state of ill in which you are.
Be sure I do not gain from it and I shall cause you pain.
But for this reason I have come, to make you see
how your son's heart was pure, that he may die with fame,
and make you see the savage passion of your wife
or, in a way, the nobleness; for she was pricked
by sting of that most hateful of the gods to us
who love a virgin life, and she desired your son.
She tried by resolution to beat Cypris down,
and then was lost, unwilling, by her nurse's craft,
who under oath informed your son of her disease.
And he, just as was right, neither was influenced
by what she said, nor, when by you he was maligned,
would break his pledged word, since his nature fears the gods.
But she, your wife, in fear lest she might be found out,
Wrote a false story down and by this trick of hers
destroyed your son, yet all the same persuaded you.

THESEUS

Alas!

64

Does the tale, Theseus, bite your heart? Yet quietly wait
and hear what follows, that you may lament still more.
You know you have three certain curses from your sire,
and one of them, you wicked man, you have misused
against your son. It might have been against a foe.
Your father, the sea's king, with honourable mind,
gave what he had to give since he had promised it.
But both to him and me your wickedness is clear.
You did not wait for guarantees or word of seers,
made no examination, nor by course of time
allowed enquiry, but, more quickly than you ought,
you laid the curse upon your son and took his life.

**THESEUS**

O lady, I am lost.

**ARTEMIS**

Your deed is dreadful. Yet
still there may be forgiveness here even for you.
It was the will of Cypris that these things should be,
to sate her rage. There is this rule among the gods,—
that none of us will check another god's desire
when it is shown. Instead we always stand aside.
Be sure that if I did not fear the power of Zeus
I never would have sunk to such a depth of shame
as to allow the death of him who is to me
dearest of men. As for your sin, first the fact
of ignorance frees you from guilt of evil thought.
And then your wife, who now is dead, poured out her
        words
of evidence so much that they persuaded you.
And on you chiefly now has broken all this ill,
but I too feel the pain. The gods do not rejoice

E                    65

when good men die. As for the wicked, we destroy
them, and their houses and the children that they have.

[*Hippolytus is carried in by his attendants.*]

CHORUS
See! Here the wretched sufferer comes.
His youthful flesh and golden hair
have lost their beauty. O what pain,
what double grief has fallen on these halls
and swooped on them from heaven!

HIPPOLYTUS
Alas! Alas!
I in my misery all disfigured
by unjust curse of an unjust father,
I am destroyed. Alas! Alas!
Through my head goes a darting anguish,
spasms leap within my brain.
Stop! Let me rest my weary body.
Hateful my chariot, hateful my horses
fed from my hand!
You have slain and destroyed me.
O, my servants, gently, I beg you
touch my bruised flesh with your hands!
Who is it standing there at my right side?
Lift me up carefully, raise me together,
me the unfortunate, me the cursed one
by fault of my father. O Zeus, do you see it?
I who was holy, I who was reverent,
I who surpassed all men in my purity,
am going to certain death under ground,
losing my life. O useless the efforts
I made out of kindness

in service to men!
Oh! Oh!
It is the pain, the pain coming over me.
Leave me to suffer!
O let Death, the Healer, come for me!
O you are killing me, doubling my pain.
How I long for a two-edged spear blade
to cut through my body
and bring my life to its rest!
O sad the curse my father laid upon me.
It is the sin of bloody ancestors.
of forefathers in ancient times, that comes
down from the past on me and will not stay.
Yet why on me all guiltless of these sins?
Alas, what should I say?
How can I free my life from this
insufferable pain?
O let the black of death and night of fate
lull me, unhappy, to my sleep!

ARTEMIS

Poor youth, how you are yoked together with your pain!
It was the goodness of your heart destroyed your life.

HIPPOLYTUS

Ha!
O heavenly breath of fragrance! Even in my pains
I feel your presence, and my body grows more light.
Is Artemis, the goddess, present in this place?

ARTEMIS

Poor youth, she is, and loves you more than all the gods.

HIPPOLYTUS

You see me, lady, and my state, my wretched state?

ARTEMIS

I see you, but my eyes are not allowed to weep.

HIPPOLYTUS

No more the huntsman for you and the serving man . . .

ARTEMIS

No more. Yet in your dying you are dear to me.

HIPPOLYTUS

No more to guard your statues or to drive your steeds.

ARTEMIS

No. It was cruel Cypris wished these things to be.

HIPPOLYTUS

Alas! I recognise the god who took my life.

ARTEMIS

Jealous of honour, angry at your living pure.

HIPPOLYTUS

Alone, I see, she has destroyed all three of us.

ARTEMIS

Yes. You, your father, and his wife, the third of you.

HIPPOLYTUS

Then I must weep too for my father's sufferings.

ARTEMIS

It was the counsel of a god deceived his mind.

HIPPOLYTUS

Unhappy father in this suffering of yours!

68

**THESEUS**

My son, I am destroyed and have no joy in life.

**HIPPOLYTUS**

More than myself, I grieve for you and your mistake.

**THESEUS**

I wish that I, my child, could die instead of you.

**HIPPOLYTUS**

Bitter the gifts your sire, Poseidon, gave to you.

**THESEUS**

I wish that it had never mounted to my lips.

**HIPPOLYTUS**

Why so? You would have killed me, angry as you were.

**THESEUS**

Yes, for the gods had cheated me of my good sense.

**HIPPOLYTUS**

Alas!
I wish the race of men had power to curse the gods.

**ARTEMIS**

Be satisfied. For no, not in the dark of earth
shall I allow, at Cypris' pleasure, rage to light
upon your body unavenged; and this because
of your godfearingness and of your noble mind.
For I shall take from her with my own hand the one
of mortals whom above all others she loves best,
and so with my unerring bow become avenged.
And now on you, unhappy one, for all your pains

I shall bestow the greatest honours in this land
of Troizen. For unmarried girls, before they wed,
shall cut their hair to do you honour. You will have
for ages long the harvest of their mourning tears.
And always among maidens there will be desire
to make their songs of you. It will not pass away
or nameless sink to silence, Phaedra's love for you.
And you, O child of aged Aigeus, I bid take
your son up in your arms and give him your embrace.
It was against your will you slew him, and it is
natural for men to err when gods point out the way.
And you, Hippolytus, I counsel not to hate
your father, for you know the fate by which you died.
Farewell! For I am not allowed to see the dead,
or stain my eye with the last gasps of dying men,
and you I see already near that evil thing.

HIPPOLYTUS

O farewell, blessed maiden, go upon your way.
Easily now you leave our long companionship.
I end my quarrel with my father, as you bid,
and as in old times also I obeyed your words.


[*Artemis goes out.*]


Ah! Ah! Already darkness settles on my eyes.
Take hold of me, my father. Keep my body straight.

THESEUS

My son, what are you doing to me in my pain?

HIPPOLYTUS

Now I am dying. Now I see the gates of hell.

70

**THESEUS**

O will you leave me here with heart unpurified?

**HIPPOLYTUS**

I will not, since I free you from the stain of blood.

**THESEUS**

What? You will set me free from guilt of shedding blood?

**HIPPOLYTUS**

I call the archer Artemis to witness it.

**THESEUS**

Dear son, how noble to your father's eyes you are.

**HIPPOLYTUS**

Pray that your true-born children may be like to me.

**THESEUS**

I weep for your good heart, your true and upright mind.

**HIPPOLYTUS**

Farewell to you too, father! O, a long farewell!

**THESEUS**

O my son, do not leave me! Summon up your strength.

**HIPPOLYTUS**

My strength is done and finished, father, and I die.
Now quickly with my garments hide away my face.

*[Hippolytus dies.]*

71

**THESEUS**

O famous bounds of Athens and of Pallas' land,
How great a man is this that you will lose! Alas!
How often, Cypris, shall I think of your ill deeds!

**CHORUS**

This is a grief that is common to all of us.
and came unexpected.
Many the tears that now will be falling,
since for great men mourning voices
still last longer.

**THE END**